THE TRUTH ABOUT
EARLY AMERICAN HISTORY

THE TRUTH ABOUT THE
AMERICAN REVOLUTION

CHARLOTTE TAYLOR

Enslow
PUBLISHING

Please visit our website, www.enslow.com. For a free color catalog of all our high-quality books, call toll free 1-800-398-2504 or fax 1-877-980-4454.

Library of Congress Cataloging-in-Publication Data
Names: Taylor, Charlotte, 1978- author.
Title: The truth about the American Revolution / Charlotte Taylor.
Description: New York : Enslow Publishing, 2023. | Series: The truth about
  early American history | Includes index.
Identifiers: LCCN 2022000269 (print) | LCCN 2022000270 (ebook) | ISBN
  9781978527881 (library binding) | ISBN 9781978527867 (paperback) | ISBN
  9781978527874 (set) | ISBN 9781978527898 (ebook)
Subjects: LCSH: United States–History–Revolution, 1775-1783–Juvenile
  literature.
Classification: LCC E208 .T37 2023 (print) | LCC E208 (ebook) | DDC
  973.3–dc23/eng/20220124
LC record available at https://lccn.loc.gov/2022000269
LC ebook record available at https://lccn.loc.gov/2022000270

Published in 2023 by
Enslow Publishing
29 E. 21st Street
New York, NY 10010
Copyright © 2023 Enslow Publishing
Portions of this work were originally authored by Shalini Saxena and published as *Paul Revere Didn't Say "The British Are Coming": Exposing Myths About the American Revolution*. All new material in this edition was authored by Charlotte Taylor.
Designer: Rachel Rising
Editor: Megan Quick

Photo credits: Cover, p. 16 Everett Collection/Shutterstock.com; Cover Brian A Jackson/Shutterstock.com; Cover, pp.1-5, 6, 8 -10 , 12, 14, 16-18, 20-24, 26-28, 30-32 pashabo/Shutterstock.com; Cover, pp.1-5, 6, 8 -10 , 12, 14, 16-18, 20-24, 26-28, 30-32 orangeberry/Shutterstock.com; Cover, pp.1-5, 6, 8 -10 , 12, 14, 16-18, 20-24, 26-28, 30-32 iulias/Shutterstock.com; Cover, pp. 1, 3, 5, 6, 9, 10, 12, 14, 17, 18, 21, 23, 24, 27, 28, 30-32 Epifantsev/Shutterstock.com; p. 4 Historical Images Archive / Alamy Stock Photo; p. 5 Syda Productions/Shutterstock.com; p. 7 https://commons.wikimedia.org/wiki/File:Boston_Tea_Party_Currier_colored.jpg; p. 8 Library of Congress Prints and Photographs Division Washington, D.C. 20540 USA https://hdl.loc.gov/loc.pnp/pp.print; p. 9 jejim/Shutterstock.com; p. 11 https://en.wikipedia.org/wiki/File:J_S_Copley_-_Paul_Revere_(cropped).jpg#/media/File:J_S_Copley_-_Paul_Revere_(cropped).jpg; p. 13 https://commons.wikimedia.org/wiki/File:The_Battle_of_Lexington.jpg; p. 15 https://commons.wikimedia.org/wiki/File:Lexington_Concord_Siege_of_Boston.jpg; p. 17 https://commons.wikimedia.org/wiki/File:Bunker_Hill_by_Pyle.jpg; p. 19 https://commons.wikimedia.org/wiki/File:The_Death_of_General_Warren_at_the_Battle_of_Bunker%27s_Hill,_June_17,_1775.jpg; p. 20 https://en.wikipedia.org/wiki/File:Declaration_of_Independence_(1819)_by_John_Trumbull.jpg; p. 21 Mike Flippo/Shutterstock.com; p. 22 https://commons.wikimedia.org/wiki/File:Molly_Pitcher_engraving.jpg; p. 23 EQRoy/Shutterstock.com; p. 25 https://commons.wikimedia.org/wiki/File:Surrender_of_General_Burgoyne.jpg; p. 26 https://commons.wikimedia.org/wiki/File:Washington_Crossing_the_Delaware_by_Emanuel_Leutze,_MMA-NYC,_1851.jpg; p. 27 https://commons.wikimedia.org/wiki/File:BattleofMonmouth.jpg; p. 29 https://commons.wikimedia.org/wiki/File:Treaty_of_Paris_by_Benjamin_West_1783.jpg.

Printed in the United States of America

Some of the images in this book illustrate individuals who are models. The depictions do not imply actual situations or events.

CPSIA compliance information: Batch #CSENS23: For further information contact Enslow Publishing, New York, New York, at 1-800-398-2504.

Find us on

CONTENTS

TRUE STORIES?

The stories of the American Revolution are filled with brave **patriots** and bloody battles. But some of what you know about America's fight for independence might not be entirely true. Did you know Paul Revere never yelled "The British are coming"? And the Declaration of Independence wasn't signed on July 4?

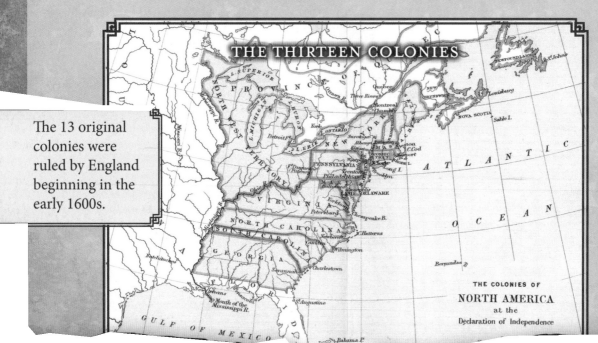

The 13 original colonies were ruled by England beginning in the early 1600s.

THE THIRTEEN COLONIES

THE COLONIES OF
NORTH AMERICA
at the
Declaration of Independence

Sometimes when stories are passed along, people change pieces of them, either by accident or on purpose. Sometimes they just don't take the time to learn the truth. But getting the facts straight about the past is the best way to understand the early history of the United States.

EXPLORE MORE!

A REVOLUTION IS NOT JUST A WAR. IT USUALLY HAPPENS WHEN A LARGE GROUP OF PEOPLE BELIEVE THAT THEY ARE BEING TREATED UNFAIRLY. THEY DECIDE TO TRY TO TAKE THE POWER AWAY FROM THEIR GOVERNMENT. THIS OFTEN HAPPENS SUDDENLY AND **VIOLENTLY**.

NOT READY TO BREAK FREE

The American Revolution did not start overnight. The colonists were not happy with England for many years. They did not like having to pay unfair taxes. They had no **representation** in the British government. But it is not true that most colonists wanted to break from England before the revolution began.

Many colonists simply wanted a say in decisions made by the British government. They **protested** to show their unhappiness with British laws and taxes. One protest was the Boston Tea Party. Many people in the colonies still were unsure if American independence was a good idea.

EXPLORE MORE!

IN 1765, ENGLAND PASSED THE STAMP ACT. IT SAID THAT COLONISTS HAD TO USE A SPECIAL STAMP ON ALL PAPERS, INCLUDING CARDS AND NEWSPAPERS. THE STAMP COST MONEY THAT WENT TO THE BRITISH GOVERNMENT. COLONISTS THOUGHT THIS WAS UNFAIR, SINCE THEY HAD NO SAY IN THE LAW'S PASSAGE.

In 1773, colonists dressed as Native Americans dumped boxes of tea from ships into the Boston Harbor. The Boston Tea Party was a protest against unfair British laws, including a tax on tea.

SOUNDING THE ALARM

Paul Revere is a famous figure of the American Revolution. He is best known for his late-night horseback ride on April 18, 1775. He warned the colonists that British troops were on their way to try to capture colonial military supplies. The story says he raced toward Concord, Massachusetts, yelling through the streets, "The British are coming!"

Paul Revere, pictured here, was a loyal patriot for many years. He helped plan the Boston Tea Party.

Revere was a brave patriot who warned the colonists of danger. But he probably didn't yell, because British soldiers might have heard him. Also, he wouldn't have said "the British" because the colonists themselves were British. He would have called British troops "regulars."

This statue of Paul Revere stands in Boston, Massachusetts.

EXPLORE MORE!

PAUL REVERE'S RIDE ON APRIL 18 WAS NOT THE FIRST TIME HE CARRIED A MESSAGE ON HORSEBACK. IN FACT, HE HAD BEEN RIDING AS A MESSENGER FOR YEARS. IN THE DAYS BEFORE TELEPHONES AND COMPUTERS, IMPORTANT NEWS AND PAPERS WERE OFTEN DELIVERED BY RIDERS.

If people have the facts wrong about Revere's midnight ride, we know who to blame. In 1861, American poet Henry Wadsworth Longfellow wrote the poem "Paul Revere's Ride." The work was not **accurate** in many ways, but it became famous, spreading Revere's story.

Because of Longfellow's poem, many people think Revere acted alone the night of his famous ride. But at least two other men, William Dawes and Samuel Prescott, also rode on the same **mission**. In fact, Revere didn't make it to Concord. The men were stopped by the British and only Prescott was able to continue all the way.

EXPLORE MORE!

LONGFELLOW WROTE HIS POEM LONG AFTER THE AMERICAN REVOLUTION. BEFORE THEN, PAUL REVERE WAS NOT WELL KNOWN OUTSIDE BOSTON. THERE, HE WAS A SILVERSMITH, MAKING ITEMS SUCH AS SPOONS AND TEA SETS. HE ALSO WORKED AS A DENTIST. ONE (UNTRUE) STORY SAYS THAT HE MADE GEORGE WASHINGTON'S FALSE TEETH.

Paul Revere was known in Boston for his fine work with gold and silver.

11

FIRST SHOT FIRED

British troops headed to Concord in April 1775 because there were weapons stored there. They hoped to destroy the weapons and stop the colonists from fighting. But on the way, the British ran into a group of American soldiers in Lexington. And it was there, not Concord, that the fight began.

Thanks to the warnings from Revere and his friends, the colonists in Lexington were ready for the British. It was not an even fight: about 700 British troops faced 77 colonists. Gunfire rang out. It is not clear who fired first: the colonists or the British soldiers.

EXPLORE MORE!

The Battle of Lexington took place on the town green just before sunrise.

Many people have written about how the American Revolution began. "The shot heard round the world" is a famous line about the start of the war. The words were written by Ralph Waldo Emerson in a poem called "Concord Hymn."

Emerson's poem is about the opening of the Battle of Concord, which happened shortly after the Battle of Lexington. But over time, many people came to believe that it was about the first shot of the revolution. Most **historians** agree that the first shot of the war was fired earlier in the day in Lexington.

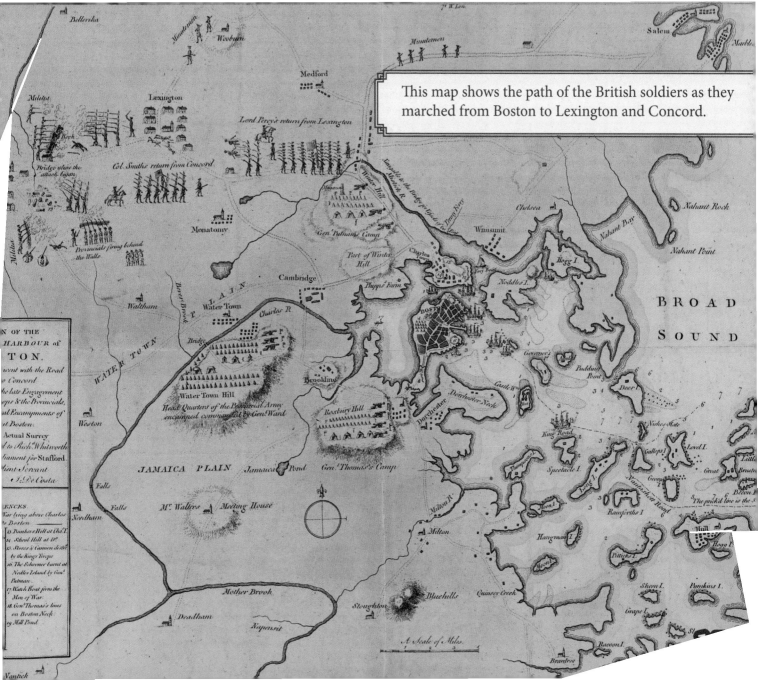

This map shows the path of the British soldiers as they marched from Boston to Lexington and Concord.

THE WRONG HILL

The Battle of Bunker Hill happened about two months after the start of the war. It was the first major battle of the American Revolution. It may be surprising to learn that it didn't actually take place on Bunker Hill.

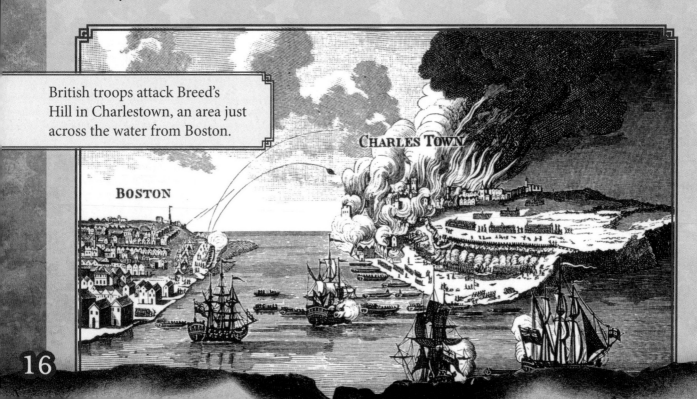

British troops attack Breed's Hill in Charlestown, an area just across the water from Boston.

CHARLES TOWN

BOSTON

On June 16, 1775, colonial forces set out to **fortify** Bunker Hill near Boston. But for some reason, their leader, William Prescott, had them fortify nearby Breed's Hill instead. Breed's Hill was lower than Bunker Hill and closer to British troops. The British fired on the colonial troops and charged up the hill, defeating the colonists.

EXPLORE MORE!

THE BOSTON AREA WAS MUCH HILLIER IN THE 1700s THAN IT IS TODAY. CONTROL OF THE HILLS WAS VERY IMPORTANT TO BOTH SIDES IN THE WAR. IT WAS EASIER TO FIRE ON THE CITY FROM ATOP THE HILLS. THEY ALSO PROVIDED A CLEAR VIEW OF SHIPS IN BOSTON HARBOR.

"THE WHITES OF THEIR EYES"

Colonists fighting at Breed's Hill did not have a huge store of powder and lead for their guns. They couldn't waste their supplies, so every shot mattered. A famous story tells of a leader ordering troops not to fire on the British until they could "see the whites of their eyes."

No one is sure who said this line. In fact, some historians are not certain that the words were said at this battle at all. And if all the colonists had held their fire until the British were that close, many more Americans would have died. The colonists probably fired from about 50 yards (45.7 m) away. That's too far to see anyone's eyes closely.

EXPLORE MORE!

THE BATTLE OF BUNKER HILL IS CALLED A VICTORY FOR THE BRITISH BECAUSE THEY WON CONTROL OF THE HILL. HOWEVER, NEARLY TWICE AS MANY BRITISH SOLDIERS DIED THERE. THE RESULT MADE THE COLONISTS FEEL THAT THEY COULD FIGHT AND WIN THE WAR.

A scene from the Battle of Bunker Hill shows the death of General Joseph Warren, a doctor who also fought in the Battles of Lexington and Concord.

THE DATE OF THE DECLARATION

More than a year after the war began, the leaders of the colonies declared, or announced, their independence from England. Every year since then, people have **celebrated** the country's freedom on Independence Day. But the vote for independence actually happened on July 2. So, what happened on the first Fourth of July?

This painting shows the Declaration of Independence being presented to the Continental Congress in 1776. The colonists were not truly independent until the end of the American Revolution.

On July 4, 1776, a group of colonists who made up the Continental Congress adopted the Declaration of Independence in Philadelphia, Pennsylvania. The **document** stated why the colonists wanted to be free from England. It was not signed on July 4. Most members of the Continental Congress signed it on August 2.

EXPLORE MORE!

JOHN ADAMS, WHO BECAME THE SECOND PRESIDENT OF THE UNITED STATES, BELIEVED THAT AMERICANS SHOULD MARK THE DAY THE COLONISTS VOTED FOR INDEPENDENCE: JULY 2. HE WROTE, "THE SECOND DAY OF JULY 1776 . . . WILL BE CELEBRATED AS THE GREAT ANNIVERSARY FESTIVAL."

THE LEGEND OF MOLLY PITCHER

Women were not allowed to fight as soldiers in the war, but they did help in many ways. Some brought pitchers, or jugs, of water to soldiers on the battlefield. Stories say Molly Hays was one of these women and that she was with her husband at the Battle of Monmouth in 1778. Some stories say that he fell and she stepped in to help work a cannon. She was called "Molly Pitcher."

Molly Hays was not linked to the story of "Molly Pitcher" until many years after her death.

However, there is no proof that the story of Molly Pitcher is true. Some historians think that it was made up based on the stories of several women. It is certainly true that many women acted bravely during the war.

IN HONOR OF

THE BATTLE OF MONMOUTH HEROINE,
MOLLY PITCHER, JUNE 28, 1778

GIFT OF THE HISTORICAL SOCIETIES OF
MONMOUTH COUNTY, N.J., D.A.R.,
MONMOUTH COUNTY HERITAGE COMMITTEE,
AND FRIENDS.
DEDICATED OCTOBER 28, 1978

EXPLORE MORE!

SOME WOMEN FOUGHT IN THE WAR BY PRETENDING TO BE MEN. OTHERS, INCLUDING LYDIA DARRAGH, MAY HAVE ACTED AS SPIES. STORIES SAY DARRAGH WATCHED THE BRITISH TROOPS FROM HER HOME AND SENT MESSAGES IN CODE TO THE PATRIOTS. SHE MAY HAVE WARNED THE AMERICANS OF A SURPRISE BRITISH ATTACK.

MISSED OPPORTUNITIES

At many points during the revolution, the colonists surprised the British with their strength. By the war's end, many said that the British could not have won. But they did have opportunities. In 1777, British general William Howe could have worked with British general John Burgoyne to take control of the Hudson River. This would have cut New England off from all the other colonies.

Instead, Howe chose to have his forces attack Philadelphia. He chose the area because the Continental Congress was there. Meanwhile, American soldiers beat Burgoyne's troops soundly in Saratoga, New York.

EXPLORE MORE!

THE PATRIOTS' VICTORY IN SARATOGA WAS A KEY MOMENT IN THE REVOLUTION. IT SHOWED FRANCE THAT AMERICANS COULD WIN THE REVOLUTION. FRANCE DECIDED TO SUPPORT THE PATRIOTS BY GIVING THEM MONEY AS WELL AS TROOPS. THIS AID FROM THE FRENCH HELPED THE AMERICANS GO ON TO WIN THE WAR.

In 1777, the British surrendered, or gave up, in Saratoga, New York. At the center of this painting are Burgoyne and American general Horatio Gates.

WASHINGTON'S WEAKNESS

When George Washington became head of the Continental army in 1775, he had never been in charge of a large army before. In fact, he made several key mistakes during the revolution. Many historians say that he was not good at planning battles.

Washington had a risky plan to cross the icy Delaware River on Christmas Eve 1776. His troops went on to victory at the Battle of Trenton in New Jersey.

America did not win the war because of Washington's talent on the battlefield. In fact, he is blamed for losses such as the British taking New York's Fort Washington and New Jersey's Fort Lee in November 1776. And it was the French who came up with the campaign that led to the 1781 Battle of Yorktown, ending the war.

EXPLORE MORE!

GEORGE WASHINGTON HAD SOME FLAWS, BUT HE WAS ALSO A BRAVE AND SMART LEADER. HE SURROUNDED HIMSELF WITH PEOPLE WHO HAD SKILLS AND KNOWLEDGE THAT HE DID NOT HAVE. HE LISTENED TO THEIR IDEAS AND USED THEM TO MAKE IMPORTANT DECISIONS.

REMEMBERING THE FIGHT

The official end of the war finally came on September 3, 1783, with the signing of the Treaty of Paris. Several years later, the U.S. Constitution was created and then ratified, or approved, by the states. The new American government officially began on March 4, 1789.

The revolution was a time of major change. Many people died in the colonists' fight to become free, and Americans still celebrate that freedom every year. Learning the truth about how the country formed is a way of honoring the people and events that led to America's independence.

EXPLORE MORE!

THE 13 ORIGINAL COLONIES DID NOT OFFICIALLY BECOME STATES AS SOON AS THE REVOLUTION ENDED. THIS HAPPENED LATER, WHEN EACH STATE APPROVED THE CONSTITUTION, STARTING IN 1787. DELAWARE WAS THE FIRST STATE TO ENTER THE UNION.

American representatives are shown at the signing of the Treaty of Paris. The painting is unfinished because the British refused to sit for it.

GLOSSARY

accurate: Free from mistakes.

celebrate: To honor with special activities.

document: A formal piece of writing.

fortify: To strengthen a place by building military defenses.

historian: Someone who studies history.

inspire: To cause someone to want to do something.

mission: A task or job that a group must perform.

patriot: A person who loves their country.

protest: To strongly oppose something.

representation: A person or group that speaks or acts for another person or group.

victory: A win over an opponent.

violent: Having to do with the use of force to harm someone.

BOOKS

Berne, Emma Carlson. *The History of the American Revolution*. Emeryville, CA: Rockridge Press, 2021.

Bolden, Jevon. *George Washington*. New York, NY: Scholastic, 2020.

Philbrick, Nathaniel. *Ben's Revolution: Benjamin Russell and the Battle of Bunker Hill*. New York, NY: Nancy Paulsen Books, 2017.

WEBSITES

DK Find Out! American Revolution

www.dkfindout.com/us/history/american-revolution/

Discover more about the people and events at the center of America's fight for freedom.

Ducksters: American Revolution

www.ducksters.com/history/american_revolution.php

Check out fascinating facts about the American Revolution.

National Geographic Kids: George Washington

kids.nationalgeographic.com/history/article/george-washington

Learn more about the Founding Father who led the American military through the revolution.

INDEX